3-14

REMARKABLE
PEOPLE

Michael Phelps
by Pamela McDowell

www.av2books.com

AV² provides enriched content that supplements and complements this book. Weigl's AV² books strive to create inspired learning and engage young minds in a total learning experience.

Your AV² Media Enhanced books come alive with...

Audio
Listen to sections of the book read aloud.

Key Words
Study vocabulary, and complete a matching word activity.

Video
Watch informative video clips.

Quizzes
Test your knowledge.

Go to **www.av2books.com**, and enter this book's unique code.

BOOK CODE

C322390

Embedded Weblinks
Gain additional information for research.

Slide Show
View images and captions, and prepare a presentation.

AV² by Weigl brings you media enhanced books that support active learning.

Try This!
Complete activities and hands-on experiments.

... and much, much more!

Published by AV² by Weigl
350 5th Avenue, 59th Floor
New York, NY 10118

www.av2books.com   www.weigl.com

Library of Congress Cataloging-in-Publication Data

McDowell, Pamela.
 Michael Phelps / Pamela McDowell.
   pages cm. -- (Remarkable people)
Includes index.
  ISBN 978-1-62127-391-2 (hardcover : alk. paper) -- ISBN 978-1-62127-397-4 (softcover : alk. paper)
1. Phelps, Michael, 1985---Juvenile literature. 2. Swimmers--United States--Biography--Juvenile literature. I. Title.
GV838.P54M32 2013
797.2'1092--dc23
 [B]
                          2012041048

Printed in the United States of America in North Mankato, Minnesota
1 2 3 4 5 6 7 8 9 0   18 17 16 15 14 13

032013
WEP300113

Editor: Heather Kissock
Design: Terry Paulhus

Photograph Credits
Weigl acknowledges Getty Images as the primary image supplier for this title. Every reasonable effort has been made to trace ownership and to obtain permission to reprint copyright material. The publishers would be pleased to have any errors or omissions brought to their attention so that they may be corrected in subsequent printings.

Contents

Who Is Michael Phelps?

Michael Phelps is one of the best-known athletes in the world. He has won 22 Olympic medals in swimming and set dozens of world records in his career. His strength lies in his ability to stay **focused** on his goal. This is an amazing achievement for a boy who was diagnosed with **attention deficit hyperactivity disorder** (ADHD) when he was nine years old.

> *"You can't put a limit on anything. The more you dream, the farther you get."*

It takes years of training and **dedication** to become an Olympic athlete. Michael swam **competitively** for 20 years. Training and competitions were the focus of his life for all that time. His mother and his coach provided support for his dream of becoming a world champion.

As a **professional** swimmer, Michael worked hard to rise to the top of his sport. Now, he works just as hard to encourage other people to participate in sports. Michael started the Michael Phelps Foundation to promote swimming and help more people become active.

Growing Up

Michael Phelps was born on June 30, 1985. He grew up in Towson, Maryland. This is a neighborhood north of Baltimore, Maryland's largest city. Michael's parents, Debbie and Fred, divorced when he was in elementary school. Michael was raised by his mother.

Even when he was young, Michael could often be found at the local pool. Here, he liked to watch his two older sisters, Hilary and Whitney, train and compete at swimming meets. Michael was full of energy, but lacked focus. His mother put him in swimming classes as a way to burn off that energy. She also felt that swimming would help him learn to remain focused on a task. Michael joined the North Baltimore Aquatic Club team in 1992.

At age seven, Michael was afraid to put his head under the water, so he swam mostly on his back. The first **stroke** he learned was the backstroke. In 1996, Coach Bob Bowman noticed that Michael had the perfect swimmer's body. He had long arms, big hands, short legs, big feet, and a long body. Bob felt that Michael could be a great swimmer, if he learned to focus.

■ Michael's mother is one of his biggest supporters. In 2009, she accompanied him to the ESPY Awards, where he took home three trophies.

Get to Know Maryland

FLOWER
Black-eyed susan

TREE
White oak

BIRD
Baltimore oriole

Pennsylvania

New Jersey

Maryland

Delaware

West Virginia

Virginia

N

| 0 | 125 Miles |
| 0 | 125 Kilometers |

Annapolis is the state capital of Maryland. It has a population of about 39,000 people.

More than one third of the nation's annual blue crab catch comes from Maryland's Chesapeake Bay.

Fort McHenry National Monument is one of Maryland's major historic attractions. It was here that Francis Scott Key wrote "The Star-Spangled Banner," a poem that later became the U.S. national anthem.

The United States Naval Academy opened in Annapolis in 1845. Navy and Marine Corps officers are still trained there today.

Think about it!

Professional athletes like Michael Phelps often focus on their goals when they are very young. Think about your own goals. Do you have a plan that will help you reach these goals? Can you break your plan into smaller steps that are easier to accomplish? What people in your family or in your community could help you work toward your goals?

Practice Makes Perfect

From a young age, Michael liked to watch the American swimmers at the Olympics. He knew that he wanted to be an Olympic swimmer someday and stayed focused on that goal. By 2000, Michael was one of the best swimmers in the United States. He surprised everyone by making the U.S. swim team when he was only 15 years old. He was the youngest swimmer to make the team in 68 years. Michael went to his first Olympic games in 2000 in Sydney, Australia, and placed fifth in the 200-meter butterfly.

Just a few months later, Michael set a world record in the 200-meter butterfly. He became the youngest male swimmer in history to set a world swimming record. In these early years, Michael often trained with athletes six or seven years older than himself.

■ The butterfly stroke is one of the most difficult to learn. Michael used his double-jointed ankles and elbows to master the technique.

It is rare for a swimmer to be talented in all four swimming strokes. Most have a specialty or a stroke that they favor, whether it is freestyle, backstroke, breaststroke, or butterfly. Michael worked hard on all his strokes and became good at all four. He was in the pool twice a day every day. He swam about 50 miles (80 kilometers) every week.

Michael competed in many different swimming events. Most of the time, his races were individual. This means that he raced alone. Sometimes, however, he competed in **relay races** with three other swimmers. His races were often different lengths, either 100, 200, or 400 meters. An Olympic-sized pool is 50 meters long, so racers must swim two, four, or eight laps of the pool to complete the race.

In 2008, Michael swam the butterfly leg of the men's 4x100m medley relay. Team USA won the event, and Michael received his record-breaking eighth gold medal of the Beijing Olympics.

Key Events

Michael became a professional swimmer when he was 16 years old. Two years later, the world caught a glimpse of what it could expect from him. He broke five world records at the 2003 World Aquatics Championships in Barcelona, Spain. Following that success, people looked forward to seeing what he would do at the 2004 Olympics in Athens, Greece. He continued his winning streak with a total of eight medals, made up of six gold and two bronze.

Four years later, Michael stunned the world. He won every race he entered at the Beijing Olympics and brought home eight gold medals. That beat the 1972 record of seven gold medals held by Mark Spitz. The years that followed were difficult for Michael, however. He lost races to teammates, and it became hard for him to stay **motivated**.

Still, Michael continued to train. Another Olympic year was approaching, and he wanted to win more medals for his country. At the 2012 Olympics in London, England, Michael made an impressive comeback. He won four gold medals and two silver medals. His total Olympic medal count was now at 22, the most medals ever won by an individual athlete.

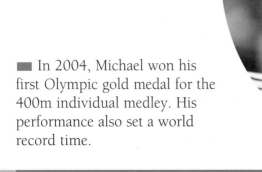

■ In 2004, Michael won his first Olympic gold medal for the 400m individual medley. His performance also set a world record time.

Thoughts from Michael

Michael has loved swimming since he was a child. Here are a few things he has said about his career and his life.

Michael discusses the importance of having goals.

"I think goals should never be easy, they should force you to work, even if they are uncomfortable..."

Michael explains how swimming makes him feel.

"Swimming is normal for me. I'm relaxed. I'm comfortable and I know my surroundings. It's my home."

Michael talks about making mistakes.

"Mom taught us to make our own decisions, but also that you have to pay for the consequences of those decisions. I'm thankful for that. I'll be the first to say I've made thousands of mistakes but I've never made the same mistake twice."

Michael talks about his Olympic goals.

"I'm going out there to try and accomplish things I have in my mind and in my heart. If I can do that, and I can have fun, that's all that matters to me."

Michael comments on winning medals.

"If I bring back only one gold (medal), people are going to say it's a disappointment. But not too many of them own an Olympic gold medal, so if I get one, I'm going to be happy."

Michael discusses mental toughness.

"I think that everything is possible as long as you put your mind to it and you put the work and time into it. I think your mind really controls everything."

What Is a Professional Athlete?

A professional athlete is a person who gets paid to play or compete in his or her sport. To become a professional athlete, a person must be very talented and determined. He or she must love the sport. Professional athletes spend as much time training as other people would spend working. Training and competing in their sport is their job.

A professional football player is paid by the organization that owns the team. Much of this money comes from fans who buy tickets to see the games. Professional swimmers, such as Michael Phelps, are paid by their **sponsors**. After the Beijing Olympics, many companies wanted to show their support for Michael. They paid him to wear their clothing and promote their products. Michael made about $6 million in one year from these sponsorships.

■ Michael is a role model whose opinion is respected by his fans. By lending his name to certain products and companies, Michael can help influence their sales.

Professional Athletes 101

Michael Jordan (1963–)

Michael Jordan was born in Brooklyn, New York, and grew up in Wilmington, North Carolina. He was always very competitive. Michael played basketball in university and won gold medals at the 1984 and 1992 Olympics as part of the U.S. basketball team. Michael was **drafted** by the Chicago Bulls and led the team to six national championships. He was inducted into the Naismith Memorial Basketball Hall of Fame in 2009.

David Beckham (1975–)

David Beckham was born in London, England. He started playing soccer when he was a child. David become a professional soccer player in 1993. For most of his career, David played with England's Manchester United team. From 2000 to 2006, he was also the captain of England's national team. David is well-known around the world for his impressive soccer skills. He is one of the world's most successful professional athletes. David now plays with France's Paris St-Germain team.

Mark Spitz (1950–)

Mark Spitz was born in Modesto, California and grew up in Honolulu, Hawai'i. He enjoyed swimming from an early age, and was competing at local swim meets by the time he was six. He was soon breaking records at the local and national levels. Mark competed in the Olympics in 1968 and 1972. He set a record in 1972, winning seven gold medals in his events. Mark retired from swimming when he was 22 years old.

Michelle Wie (1989–)

Michelle Wie was born in Honolulu, Hawai'i, in 1989. At 10 years of age, she became the youngest player ever to qualify for a United States Golf Association (USGA) amateur championship. She won the U.S. Women's Amateur Public Links Championship when she was only 13 years old. This made her the youngest person ever to win an adult USGA championship. Michelle turned professional at age 15. She earned $20 million in her first year as a professional golfer. Michelle won her first professional tournament in 2009.

Sponsorships and Endorsements

Besides sponsorships, professional athletes can also make money through endorsements. An endorsement is very similar to a sponsorship. Both involve a **contract** between the athlete and a company. A sponsor funds an athlete while he or she focuses on his or her sport. In return, the athlete agrees to promote the sponsor when in public. The athlete may wear the company's logo on his or her clothing, for example. When an athlete endorses a company, he or she is paid to promote and use the company's products. These products may or may not be directly related to the athlete's sport.

Influences

The two people who influenced Michael the most throughout his swimming career were his coach and his mother. Bob Bowman was Michael's coach for 16 years. Over that time, Bob learned how to motivate Michael. He knew it was important to keep Michael interested in improving his skills. Bob set up a variety of training exercises so that Michael did not become bored with practicing.

Debbie Phelps showed her son that hard work and determination can lead to success. Following her divorce, Debbie went back to school and studied to become a school principal. All the while, she made sure that she spent time with her children and encouraged their interests. This continued after she graduated. Even though she was working full-time as a school principal, she managed to drive Michael to his early morning practices and attend his swim meets.

■ Over the years, Bob has shared in Michael's many successes. The two men consider themselves to be collaborators and partners.

As a competitor, Michael's main goal was to be the best at what he did. He wanted to swim faster than the other swimmers in the pool, and he wanted to win more medals than other athletes. When people said that beating someone's record was impossible, Michael strove to beat the record. Such was the case when Michael decided to beat Mark Spitz's record of seven Olympic gold medals. When an Australian swimmer named Ian Thorpe declared that no one would ever beat Spitz's record, Michael took up the challenge. Before the Beijing Olympics, he memorized Thorpe's statement and used it to motivate him in his races.

PHELPS' FAMILY

Michael remains close to his mother and two sisters. All three children continue to enjoy athletics. Hilary and Whitney were both competitive swimmers. Whitney tried out for the Olympic team when she was 15, but injuries prevented her from continuing. Hilary swam on her college team. Today, Whitney has started running in marathons.

■ Michael and his sisters encourage each other to become better athletes. When Whitney began preparing for the New York City Marathon in 2012, Michael and Hilary trained with her in the pool.

Overcoming Obstacles

After his success at the Beijing Olympics, Michael found it difficult to stay motivated. Training became a burden. He simply did not feel like working as hard as he had before the games. Michael started to skip workouts and training sessions. He gained 25 pounds (11 kilograms) because he was not exercising regularly.

Eventually, Michael realized that his actions were not helping his career. He knew he wanted to continue swimming competitively and felt that he had not yet reached his full **potential**. He was not ready to quit swimming. He realized that it was time for him to get focused again. Michael sat down and wrote out his goals, like he had every year since he was 11 years old. Then, he began working on a plan to achieve them. One of his main goals was competing at the 2012 Olympics in London.

■ Michael worked hard to get in shape for the London Olympics. He trained on the rings to build his upper body strength.

To prepare for the London Olympics, Michael focused on exercises that built up his strength and **stamina**. Weight training became an important part of his training. He did power lifts and box jumps to increase his power jumping off the block at the start of a race. He practiced kicking in deep water while holding a 15-pound (7-kg) weight over his head. Michael even dragged a parachute through the water to improve his swimming strength. He would also watch videos of his races to look for ways to improve.

By the time Michael arrived in London, he was fit and focused. His success at the games proved that his hard work had been worth the effort. Still, Michael knew that he was changing. Swimming had been his life for a long time. He wanted to explore other interests and see where they took him. Shortly after the Olympics, Michael retired from professional swimming.

■ Michael was a proud member of Team USA in 2012. He won gold in the men's 4x100m medley relay, along with teammates Brendan Hansen, Matthew Grevers, and Nathan Adrian.

Achievements and Successes

Michael set many records during his 20-year swimming career. He is even a world record holder for being the swimmer with the most world records. Michael has won 71 medals in international long-course competitions, including the Olympics, World Championships, and Pan Pacific Championships. Of those, 57 are gold medals.

This success has earned Michael recognition outside of the swimming pool. *Swimming World* magazine has named him the World Swimmer of the Year Award seven times. *Sports Illustrated* magazine named him Sportsman of the Year after his showing at the Beijing Olympics. Towson, Maryland even recognized Michael's achievements by naming a street after him. Michael Phelps Way is near the high school he attended, Towson High School.

■ Michael was given a special award when he became the most decorated Olympian of all time. Soviet gymnast Larisa Latynina held the previous record, with 18 Olympic medals.

Michael worked hard to achieve success for himself and for Team USA. His greatest achievement, though, may be in the way he has brought attention to the sport of swimming. He has made swimming exciting and has shown other athletes that it is possible to do more with their lives. Michael has inspired children to join swim clubs and challenged his competitors to swim in different races, not just their specialty strokes. He has set an example for other athletes to follow in working toward their goals.

HELPING OTHERS

When Michael won eight gold medals at the Beijing Olympics, one of his sponsors paid him a $1 million bonus. Michael used this money to establish a foundation that promotes healthy and active living, especially for children. The main purpose of the Michael Phelps Foundation is to help the sport of swimming grow among Americans. The foundation gives funding to talented swimmers who cannot pay for the programs they need. Michael holds a golf tournament each year to raise money for the foundation. He plans to spend more time working at the foundation now that he has retired from swimming.

Write a Biography

A person's life story can be the subject of a book. This kind of book is called a biography. Biographies describe the lives of remarkable people, such as those who have achieved great success or have done important things to help others. These people may be alive today, or they may have lived many years ago. Reading a biography can help you learn more about a remarkable person.

At school, you might be asked to write a biography. First, decide who you want to write about. You can choose a professional athlete, such as Michael Phelps, or any other person. Then, find out if your library has any books about this person. Learn as much as you can about him or her. Write down the key events in this person's life. What was this person's childhood like? What has he or she accomplished? What are his or her goals? What makes this person special or unusual?

A concept web is a useful research tool. Read the questions in the following concept web. Answer the questions in your notebook. Your answers will help you write a biography.

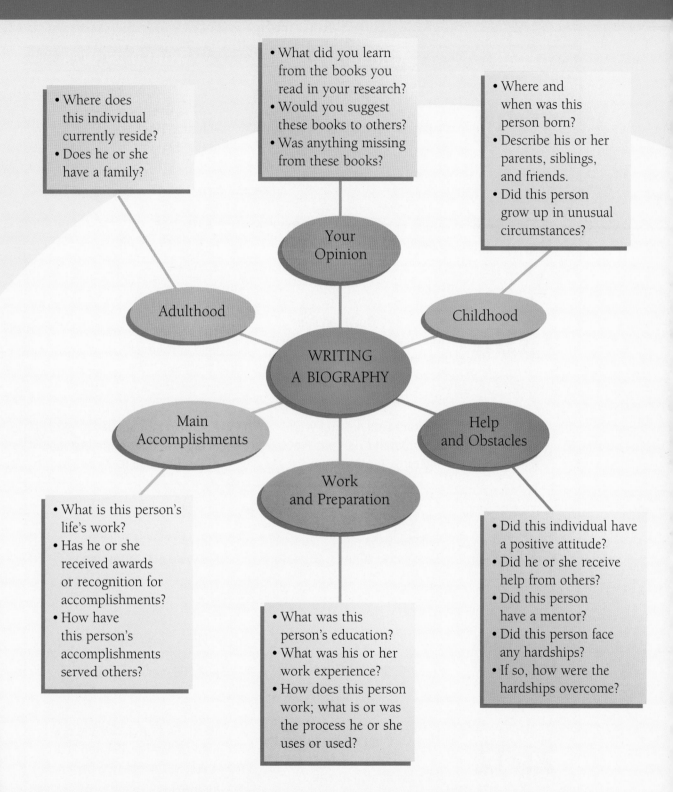

- What did you learn from the books you read in your research?
- Would you suggest these books to others?
- Was anything missing from these books?

- Where does this individual currently reside?
- Does he or she have a family?

- Where and when was this person born?
- Describe his or her parents, siblings, and friends.
- Did this person grow up in unusual circumstances?

Your Opinion

Adulthood

Childhood

WRITING A BIOGRAPHY

Main Accomplishments

Help and Obstacles

Work and Preparation

- What is this person's life's work?
- Has he or she received awards or recognition for accomplishments?
- How have this person's accomplishments served others?

- What was this person's education?
- What was his or her work experience?
- How does this person work; what is or was the process he or she uses or used?

- Did this individual have a positive attitude?
- Did he or she receive help from others?
- Did this person have a mentor?
- Did this person face any hardships?
- If so, how were the hardships overcome?

Timeline

YEAR	MICHAEL PHELPS	WORLD EVENTS
1985	Michael Phelps is born on June 30.	Wayne Gretzky is the National Hockey League's leading scorer.
1992	Michael joins the North Baltimore Aquatic Club.	The Toronto Blue Jays win baseball's World Series.
1996	Coach Bob Bowman sees Michael's potential and becomes his swim coach.	The Summer Olympics are held in Atlanta, Georgia.
2001	Michael sets his first world record in the 200-meter butterfly and turns professional.	NASCAR's Dale Earnhardt dies in a crash during the last lap of the Daytona 500.
2004	Michael wins eight medals at the Olympics in Athens, Greece.	Phil Mickelson wins the Masters golf tournament.
2008	Michael breaks Mark Spitz's record, winning eight gold medals at the Beijing Olympics.	Jamaican sprinter Usain Bolt sets world records in the 100 and 200 meter sprints.
2012	After winning six medals at the London Olympics, Michael retires from swimming at age 27.	Usain Bolt becomes the first man to win the 100 and 200 meter sprints at two Olympics in a row.

Key Words

attention deficit hyperactivity disorder: a condition in which a person is unable to pay attention to a task for a steady period and is easily distracted

competitively: in a way that strives for quality over others

contract: a written agreement to do something

dedication: great focus on a purpose or goal

drafted: selected to play for a professional team

focused: the state of paying close or narrow attention to something

motivated: encouraged to take action

potential: capable of becoming something

professional: making money by doing something that other people do for fun

relay races: races between two or more teams. Each team member goes a certain distance and then is replaced by another team member.

sponsors: individuals or organizations that finance a project or an event carried out by another person or group

stamina: the strength to resist or withstand illness, fatigue, or hardship

stroke: a method of moving the arms and legs to push against the water and propel the swimmer forward. There are four basic strokes in professional swimming. These are the backstroke, breaststroke, butterfly, and freestyle.

Index

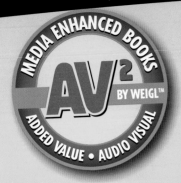

Log on to www.av2books.com

AV² by Weigl brings you media enhanced books that support active learning. Go to www.av2books.com, and enter the special code found on page 2 of this book. You will gain access to enriched and enhanced content that supplements and complements this book. Content includes video, audio, weblinks, quizzes, a slide show, and activities.

AV² Online Navigation

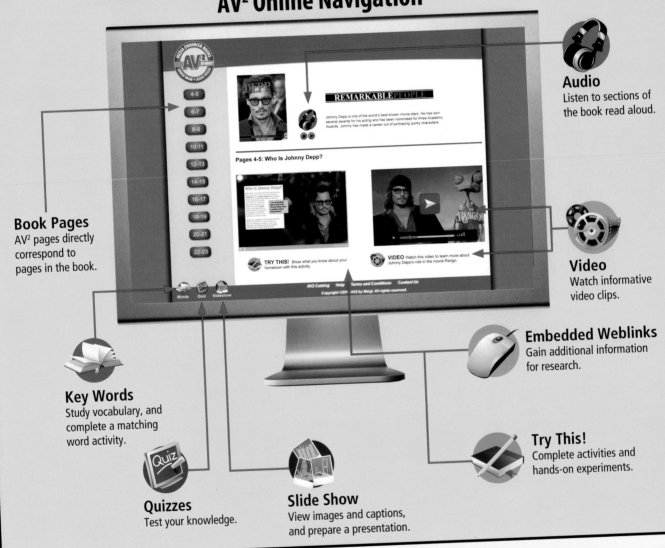

Audio
Listen to sections of the book read aloud.

Book Pages
AV² pages directly correspond to pages in the book.

Video
Watch informative video clips.

Key Words
Study vocabulary, and complete a matching word activity.

Embedded Weblinks
Gain additional information for research.

Try This!
Complete activities and hands-on experiments.

Quizzes
Test your knowledge.

Slide Show
View images and captions, and prepare a presentation.

AV² was built to bridge the gap between print and digital. We encourage you to tell us what you like and what you want to see in the future.

Sign up to be an AV² Ambassador at www.av2books.com/ambassador.

Due to the dynamic nature of the Internet, some of the URLs and activities provided as part of AV² by Weigl may have changed or ceased to exist. AV² by Weigl accepts no responsibility for any such changes. All media enhanced books are regularly monitored to update addresses and sites in a timely manner. Contact AV² by Weigl at 1-866-649-3445 or av2books@weigl.com with any questions, comments, or feedback.